IMAGES
of America

COAST GUARD
BASE ELIZABETH CITY

A HH-60J Jayhawk and HC-130H Hercules fly in formation past the Cape Hatteras Lighthouse in 1993, prior to the light's relocation away from the approaching Atlantic Ocean. The Jayhawk and Hercules have been stationed at Coast Guard Air Station Elizabeth City since 1993 and 1959, respectively. (U.S. Coast Guard.)

IMAGES
of America

COAST GUARD
BASE ELIZABETH CITY

Air Station Elizabeth City Wardroom

Copyright © 2005 by Air Station Elizabeth City Wardroom
ISBN 0-7385-1836-0

Published by Arcadia Publishing
Charleston SC, Chicago IL, Portsmouth NH, San Francisco CA

Printed in Great Britain

Library of Congress Catalog Card Number: 2005926949

For all general information contact Arcadia Publishing at:
Telephone 843-853-2070
Fax 843-853-0044
E-mail sales@arcadiapublishing.com
For customer service and orders:
Toll-Free 1-888-313-2665

Visit us on the internet at http://www.arcadiapublishing.com

CG1487, a HH-3F, hovers low to the water practicing rescue swimmer deployments. The Sikorsky H-3 Pelican served the U.S. Coast Guard from 1968 through 1994. (U.S. Coast Guard.)

CONTENTS

ACKNOWLEDGMENTS

The authors wish to acknowledge the outstanding support and patience of all the individuals who took their time to make a contribution to *Coast Guard Base Elizabeth City*. The individuals who stand out most are the pilots and aircrew who make up the Ancient Order of the Pterodactyl, who graciously opened their photo archive to help begin the project. The Coast Guard Historian's Office and their very informative Web site were great helps in running down facts. Thank you to Capt. Sperry Storm for his openness and willingness to volunteer his time, and to the individuals who trustingly lent us their own personal pictures for this project, for many of them treasured mementos of great careers: Comdr. Jay Taylor, Jim Mahoney, CWO (Chief Warrant Officer) Gerry Watts, CWO Michael Proctor, AETC (Aviation Electrical Technician Chief) Wes Fleming, Maggi Cathey, Lt. Craig Neubecker, James Doughty, and Gene Cooper. Thank you to Capt. Rod Ansley, commanding officer of Air Station Elizabeth City, for his strong support of this project despite its ups and downs, and to Adam Latham and the folks at Arcadia Publishing for their patience and faith in its completion.

The greatest debt of thanks belongs to the enlisted aircrew of Air Station Elizabeth City, the Aircraft Repair and Supply Center, and the Aviation Technical Training Center, without whom Coast Guard aviation would have never reached the heights it has attained and could never even dream of the future it has; without them this book would not have been possible.

INTRODUCTION

Northeast North Carolina has played a major role in aviation since the Wright Brothers used Elizabeth City, North Carolina, as a final jumping-off point for their journey from Dayton to Kitty Hawk in 1903. The Coast Guard Base in Elizabeth City continues that tradition. Beginning in 1939 and continuing through the present day, the only airport owned and operated by the United States Coast Guard has been the crown jewel of Coast Guard aviation. Built in 1939 as part of the military buildup for the coming world war, the base spent its first five years under the operational and administrative control of the U.S. Navy. During the war years, the base population reached 8,500 personnel, and the base was a major maintenance depot for flying boats. The Air Station was responsible for antisubmarine and Search and Rescue (SAR) for the major shipping lanes around the Outer Banks of North Carolina, leading up to the navy base in Norfolk, Virginia. Following the end of World War II, control of the base reverted back to the Coast Guard, which made immediate use of the extensive maintenance facilities by creating the Aircraft Repair and Supply Base (AR&SB) in 1947. The Coast Guard led the way into the future of SAR with the first use of the helicopter, and Elizabeth City was on the forefront as home to the Rotary Wing Development Squadron, led by the legendary Comdr. Frank "Swede" Erickson. The jump to the helicopter was not immediate, nor done willingly by the Coast Guard aviation establishment. One of the Air Station's commanding officers, Capt. Donald B. MacDairmid, was the champion of the flying boat and fought Erickson at almost every turn as to which aircraft would be the future of SAR. The 1950s and early 1960s were the golden age of flying boats as instruments of SAR, and Elizabeth City and the surrounding area was the center point of this golden age. The U.S. Navy's jet flying boat program was designated for basing at nearby Harvey Point before being cancelled.

By the mid-1960s, AR&SB had built a reputation as a premier maintenance rework facility. All U.S. Coast Guard aircraft came through the two huge hangars on the east end of the 880-acre complex. HO-4S, HH-52, and HH-3 helicopters, as well as Grumman HU-16s, Fairchild C-123s, and Lockheed C-130s, were all disassembled and built back up in a comprehensive program that ensured the long life of the airframes. The base has also been the "boot camp" for all of Coast Guard aviation's enlisted rates. In the 1970s, the Aviation Technical Training Center (ATTC) consolidated all aircrew rate training in one complex of buildings. The 1970s also saw the creation of the National Strike Force, as the Coast Guard once again led the way in preparedness for environmental disasters by creating a quick-reaction force that would be able to immediately respond to marine disasters to mitigate their effects on the environment. Today the Air Station's C-130 Hercules aircraft carry out the spills of national significance mission in support of the

National Strike Force Coordination Center. Elizabeth City's Coast Guard Base continues to lead the service into the future, as the present Aircraft Repair and Supply Center (AR&SC) is a Department of Homeland Security–recognized "center of excellence" carrying out major depot-level maintenance for every Coast Guard airframe as well as U.S. Air Force helicopters. The airport is now home to the Air Station, executing over 1,000 SAR, logistics, and homeland security missions a year with nine helicopters and airplanes and the C-130J Aircraft Program Office, which is implementing the new J-model C-130 with six airplanes.

One

BEGINNINGS
1939–1960

Hangar 49 is shown in 1940, shortly before the Coast Guard Base became a foundation of aircraft research and development for the U.S. Navy during World War II. Note the rounded curves of the building's face and the art-deco style the designers tried to capture. A Grumman Widgeon and the Coast Guard's only version of a RQ-1 electronics test aircraft, a Stinson Reliant, are parked on the right side of the hangar door. According to Coast Guard records, the Stinson was based in Cape May, New Jersey, at this time. (U.S. Government.)

Pictured here is an aerial view of the 880-acre base complex some time during World War II. The Air Station's hangar is visible in the center right of the picture, as well as the present-day Aircraft Repair and Supply Hangars in the lower right. The U.S. Navy had greatly expanded operations in Elizabeth City, basing over 100 aircraft there and over 8,000 personnel. (U.S. Government.)

A Hall PH-2 seaplane is pushed by ground crew to the seaplane ramp for a patrol shortly after the Air Base's opening in 1940. The smaller seaplane on the left is a Grumman Widgeon, which was the only Coast Guard aircraft in World War II to be officially credited with a solo kill of a German U-boat. Two Fairchild JK-1 land-based planes are also visible in the front of the hangar. (U.S. Coast Guard.)

Fairchild J2K-1s are lined up outside of Hangar 49 in 1940. The hangar was built in 1938–1939; notice the art-deco design of the building and large glass panels all around the hangar. (U.S. Coast Guard.)

In wartime Elizabeth City, aviation cadets are given a taste of tear gas during training. Driven home by the lessons of World War I, gas drills were given on little or no notice. (U.S. Coast Guard.)

Two Vought OSU2 Kingfishers head out to sea to search for German U-boats off the Outer Banks. Elizabeth City aircraft did a large part of the antisubmarine patrols for the major convoys that traveled between the U.S. Navy bases in Charleston, South Carolina, and Norfolk, Virginia. (U.S. Coast Guard.)

Survivors of the Coast Guard's sinking cutters *Bedloe* and *Jackson* are rescued by a Vought OSU2 Kingfisher from Elizabeth City. The major wartime duties of the base were basic aviation training, Search and Rescue (SAR), and antisubmarine patrol for the mid-Atlantic region. The Kingfisher has the wartime blue camouflage and U.S. Navy markings but was flown and maintained by U.S. Coast Guard crews. (U.S. Coast Guard.)

This is the transfer of the survivors of the disaster that claimed the U.S. Coast Guard cutters *Bedloe* and *Jackson*. The cutters were two 125-foot-long patrol boats of 232 tons displacement lost off Cape Hatteras in a hurricane in September 1944. Cutter *Jackson* lost 21 men in this tragedy. This episode served as a reminder that the German Navy was not always the most dangerous threat on the ocean. (U.S. Coast Guard.)

13

This is a close-up of the Vought OSU2 Kingfisher on patrol. Built by the Vought and Sikorsky companies during World War II, the Kingfisher had a crew of two, a pilot and observer; two .30-caliber machine guns, one forward firing, the other rear; and armament stations to mount either two 100-pound bombs or a single 325-pound depth charge. A single 100-pounder is visible under the left wing. (U.S. Coast Guard.)

Lieutenant Perry and Radioman First Class Ford are congratulated by the Air Station's commanding officer, Richard Burke, for a successful patrol that claimed destruction of a German U-boat in the spring of 1943. (U.S. Coast Guard.)

Perry and Ford point to the silhouette of a U-boat in May 1943, after a successful patrol. The location of Elizabeth City was important to the war effort because the unit's patrol area sat astride the major north-south domestic maritime convoy routes and just outside the largest naval base on the East Coast at Norfolk, Virginia. (U.S. Coast Guard.)

A SNJ-6 Texan is pushed into Hangar 49 in 1945. The Texan was used by the Coast Guard for proficiency flying and general administration duties. Also note that the AR&SB uses "USCG" on the right wing to identify the aircraft. (U.S. Coast Guard.)

Cadet Altekruse sits in an SNJ acting as a brake-rider while the aircraft is towed into parking for maintenance. (U.S. Coast Guard.)

The future of U.S. Coast Guard aviation was changing quickly in 1945, when this Sikorsky HNS helicopter was conducting training in a hover over the Dismal Swamp. The Coast Guard Base in Elizabeth City would be the center of the revolution as home to the Helicopter Experimental Test Squadron, headed by the legendary Comdr. Frank "Swede" Erickson. (U.S. Coast Guard.)

One of the AR&SB hangars was the stage for the depot-level maintenance for a PBM-4 Mariner (far left), two PB-1Gs (the Coast Guard version of the B-17 Flying Fortress, at left and right), and a Grumman Widgeon (center). Depot-level maintenance required a full aircraft dismantling and buildup to ensure airframe longevity and mechanical soundness. (U.S. Coast Guard.)

This view of the airport from the eastern perimeter fence shows the approach end of runways 25 and 28. Runway 25 is now Golf Taxiway, and Runway 28 is still the airport's main runway. (U.S. Coast Guard.)

Here is the flight line at the Air Station in 1946. Seemingly waiting for the huge growth that would occur at Elizabeth City in the coming years, four PB-1s sit next to a PBM-3, while AR&SB's hangars loom in the distance. (U.S. Coast Guard Pterodactyls.)

This is a close-up of the Elizabeth City airport control tower in 1946. Staffed by military personnel, the tower directed traffic for the Air Station's operational AR&SB test flights and the many U.S. Navy training flights that used the field for practice landings. (U.S. Coast Guard.)

A Martin PBM-3 Mariner is readied for a water take-off on the seaplane ramp in 1946. The diverse nature of the U.S. Coast Guard's aircraft inventory during this period is also illustrated by the PBY Catalina in the top left behind another Mariner, while a small Bell helicopter prepares for takeoff. Also pictured are two Lockheed twin-engine aircraft used for logistics transport. (U.S. Coast Guard.)

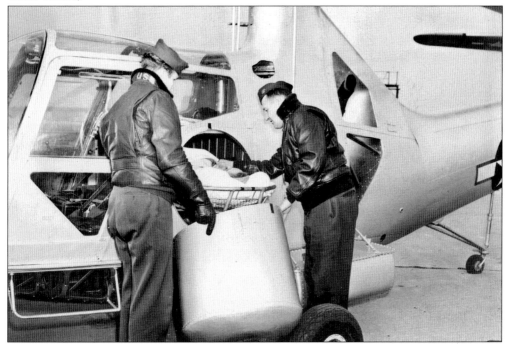

Officers from the Rotary Wing Development Unit, based in Elizabeth City, check the fit of one of their innovations, the Stretcher Blister, which allowed safer transport of a severely injured individual without the stresses of being outside of the skin of the helicopter. (U.S. Coast Guard.)

The helicopters begin to make their mark. The Sikorsky HOS-1 Hoverfly is used for a helicopter medical evacuation in late 1947. Due to the isolation of the Outer Banks, North Carolina, the helicopter represented a huge leap forward in the ability to get individuals needing urgent medical care to the appropriate hospital. (U.S. Coast Guard.)

Coast Guard personnel work to take the Stretcher Blister off an HOS-1 prior to offloading the patient at Elizabeth City. Note the lack of protective equipment on the helicopter pilot compared to today's personnel. (U.S. Coast Guard.)

The medivac (emergency medical evacuation) patient is taken from the Hoverfly helicopter to a waiting ambulance for further care. Then as now, the helicopter's ability to land almost everywhere has a positive effect on any number of dire situations and attracts attention. Note the young boys on the right following the action. (U.S. Coast Guard.)

A U.S. Navy Beech JRB-4 sits on the Coast Guard ramp in 1952. The Martin PBM-4 parked next to it gives an excellent view of the nose cargo door. (Note the missing star on the insignia.) (James Doughty.)

This is a view of the west side of Hangar 49 in 1952. The small control tower was staffed by U.S. Coast Guard personnel for over 40 years. There is also a good view of the ground-service equipment garages at the base of the building. The garages are now office space. (James Doughty.)

A Piasecki HRP-1, or Flying Banana, sits on the AR&SB ramp awaiting its next flight while a HO3S-1G flies overhead. An R-5C, also designated the C-46 Commando, sits in the background. The Coast Guard used the R-5C as an executive transport aircraft for U.S. Coast Guard headquarters personnel. The Flying Banana had a crew of two and could carry eight survivors. (U.S. Coast Guard.)

Pictured here is Hangar 49 in 1949. The tail of a Flying Banana is seen in the hangar, as well as the high-frequency radio antennae used by the Rescue Coordination Center to execute SAR operations. (U.S. Coast Guard.)

This is an aerial picture of the Air Station in 1948. You can see the development over the years, and many of these buildings are still in use today. There is an array of aircraft on the ramp, as the Coast Guard absorbed many surplus aircraft from other services following World War II. (U.S. Coast Guard Pterodactyls.)

23

Shown here is a Beech JRB-4 used by the Coast Guard from 1943 to 1958. Seven of these Beechcraft C-45-type airplanes were used by the Coast Guard, mainly for administrative flights. A specially equipped model was used to assist the Coast and Geodetic Survey in harbor mapping and photography. This aircraft was assigned to Air Station Elizabeth City and was used for administrative and proficiency flights. (U.S. Coast Guard.)

The HO-3S Dragonfly was one of the first helicopters that the Rotary Wing Development Squadron, led by Comdr. Frank Erickson, would use to push helicopter operations into a Coast Guard aviation community that was the domain of the flying boat. The Dragonfly pictured is testing emergency flotation bags attached to the landing gear. Float bags were just one of the many innovations that would revolutionize U.S. Coast Guard aviation and helicopter operations in general. (U.S. Coast Guard.)

This aerial picture was taken in 1949, and one quickly notices the increased development of the base. This growth can be attributed to the navy's use of the field during World War II. The ramp in the top left corner is now home to the Aircraft Repair and Supply Center, where all Coast Guard aircraft come for depot maintenance, and the ramp in the center is the Air Station ramp. (U.S. Coast Guard.)

This R-5D is parked at the Coast Guard Aviation Detachment (AvDet) in Argentia, Newfoundland, as part of the International Ice Patrol in late 1959. The AvDet in Argentia was supported by maintenance and flight crews from Elizabeth City during the spring and summer months, when the North Atlantic shipping lanes would experience the greatest threat from wayward icebergs. (U.S. Coast Guard Pterodactyls.)

A Douglas R-4D sits on the AR&SB ramp in the mid-1950s. The Coast Guard version of the DC-3 was used for logistics transport and administrative flying. The paint job on this aircraft is slightly different from the normal fleet aircraft as it had "U.S. Coast Guard" in large, block letters denoting it as a VIP transport as well. (U.S. Coast Guard.)

Pictured in this close-up is an experimental bomb used to break up icebergs for the International Ice Patrol. The bomb is mounted on a wing rack of a HU-16 Albatross, while an R-5D flies in formation with the test aircraft. This method did not yield the expected results and was eventually shelved. (U.S. Coast Guard.)

The Stinson OY-1 or L-5 Sentinel was used by the Coast Guard from 1948 to 1962 primarily for law enforcement. Specifically, these sturdy little planes saw action as spotters for the alcohol tax unit of the Treasury Department helping the "Revenoors" in locating illegal stills. Eight of these airplanes were based at Elizabeth City and served in the Mid-Atlantic Coastal Moonshine Area, an area with a high volume of illicit moonshine activity. These planes were stationed at Elizabeth City but would operate at other locations on temporary duty. On February 11, 1958, Lt. (jg) E. A. McGee, a Coast Guard pilot, was killed in Texas after hitting the treetops while searching for an illicit still. His passenger, a Treasury agent, survived the crash. The current duty crew berthing at the Air Station is named in McGee's honor. (U.S. Coast Guard.)

Pictured are Hanger 49 and the seaplane ramp in 1957; a Martin P5M-2G Marlin is taxiing out to the Pasquotank River for a flight. (U.S. Coast Guard.)

Here is an opposite view of the seaplane ramp with the Marlin taxiing for a water takeoff. The Air Station's administration building, paraloft, and high-frequency antennas for the Rescue Coordination Center are visible in the center right. (U.S. Coast Guard.)

The Coast Guard acquired the PB-1G (B-17) Flying Fortress as a direct result of war surplus. The aircraft greatly improved the Coast Guard's long-range, air-sea rescue capabilities. Eighteen PB-1Gs were transferred from the U.S. Air Force in September 1946. The converted B-17s became the most successful of all adapted long-range search aircraft. They were used until 1957 for the International Ice Patrol and coastal mapping surveys, as well. (U.S. Coast Guard.)

On the Air Station ramp in 1957, two Martin P5Ms, one a P5M-2G (on the seaplane ramp), the other a P5M-1G (being serviced), sit alongside a Grumman J-4F Widgeon, a PB-1G, and a navy AD-1 Skyraider. A lone HO-4S is standing at SAR ready opposite the fixed-wing aircraft. (U.S. Coast Guard.)

The Aircraft Repair and Supply Base made good use of the extensive aviation depot facilities left by the navy following World War II. Hangar 78 is pictured here; at the time of this picture, it was a major rework facility for the HU-16 Goat. (U.S. Coast Guard.)

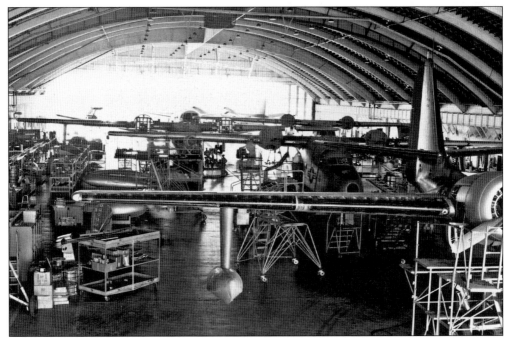

Four HU-16E Albatrosses are lined up in the hangar at AR&SB. The aircraft were stripped down, which included removing the engines, and given a thorough inspection and maintenance overhaul. In the background, an R-4D can be seen waiting its turn in the maintenance cycle. (U.S. Coast Guard.)

Coast Guard HU-16s continue their progression through the AR&SB hangar. Here, the paint has been stripped and the airframe is inspected. Once the overhaul is complete, a fresh coat of paint will be applied. (U.S. Coast Guard.)

The advent of helicopter operations into Coast Guard aviation led to many different types of aircraft showing up on the ramp of AR&SB. A Kaman HK-1 is parked in front of one of the temporary hangars at the present-day location of the Aviation Technical Training Center (ATTC). The HK-1 has two contra-rotating main rotors, negating the need for a tail rotor. (U.S. Coast Guard.)

Another helicopter evaluated by the Coast Guard was the Bell HTL-1; this first version of the venerable Bell 47 utility helicopter saw great service with the U.S. Army in Korea and numerous civilian operations. It was tested by the Elizabeth City–based Rotary Wing Development Squadron in the late 1940s. Following their initial evaluation in Elizabeth City, the service acquired two of the aircraft and stationed them at Traverse City, Michigan, and Miami, Florida. (U.S. Coast Guard.)

The Sikorsky HO-4, also known as the S-55, was used by the Coast Guard from 1951 to 1966. The radial-engine helicopter was the first to make great use of the U.S. Coast Guard–developed rescue basket, hanging off the right side of the helicopter. This basket design is essentially unchanged and is still in use on all Coast Guard SAR helicopters. (U.S. Coast Guard.)

An Air Station HO-4S conducts day hoisting training with the unit aviation training boat. Note the distinct lack of personal protective equipment on the boat crew; present-day U.S. Coast Guard boat crews are equipped with float coats, protective helmets, and insulated clothing. (U.S. Coast Guard.)

An HO-4S taxis out for a training flight in 1952. The radial-powered Sikorsky helicopter was the foundation of rotary-wing Coast Guard operations in the early years. (U.S. Coast Guard.)

An HO-4S begins a major depot-level maintenance period at the Aircraft Repair and Supply Center (AR&SC) in the late 1950s. (U.S. Coast Guard.)

Shown here is the AR&SC Hangar 1 (present-day Hangar 78) in 1958. The two large hangars were home to the maintenance of every U.S. Coast Guard airframe. (U.S. Coast Guard.)

The 1950s were the heyday for the service's large flying boats. They represented the backbone of oceangoing search and rescue because of their ability to fly far offshore and, under certain circumstances, land to pick up survivors. The Martin P-5M Marlin is shown flying over northeast North Carolina on a training flight from Elizabeth City. The Marlin could make use of the Jet Assisted Takeoff (JATO) system to take off at higher gross weights. (U.S. Coast Guard.)

In 1957, Elizabeth City was the site of the retirement of the last PB-1G (B-17) in U.S. military service. The Flying Fortress had served the Coast Guard in many different roles including long-range SAR, International Ice Patrol, and U.S. Geodetic Survey service. The aircraft provided an excellent platform for the first-generation surface-search radars and could deploy a life raft to assist survivors. The future beckoned, though, and the aircraft was retired in favor of newer aircraft like the HU-16 Albatross and C-130 Hercules. (U.S. Coast Guard.)

This is an aerial view of the Air Station from Runway 10 looking north in 1960. The building at the top left currently is home to the rescue swimmer school's pool, started in Elizabeth City in the early 1980s. The building closest to the runway on the left side has since been torn down, but the other buildings are still in use. (U.S. Coast Guard.)

The Lockheed HC-130B/E/H Hercules (1957–present) was the Coast Guard's first step into jet engine–powered aircraft. The Hercules has proven to be an outstanding search platform. Used on a variety of missions such as search and rescue, international ice patrol, and law enforcement, the "Herc" has a range of 2,100 miles and a cruise speed of 280 knots. The aircraft were purchased on Air Force contracts for the Coast Guard. (U.S. Coast Guard.)

Two

GOATS, HERCS, AND PELICANS
1961–1975

In Hanger 49 during the 1960s, maintenance is performed on an HH-52A Sea Guard and an HU-16 Albatross or Goat. The HH-52A was the Coast Guard's first amphibious helicopter; the Sea Guard was purchased in July 1962. It had a single, 845-shaft-horsepower, turbo-shaft engine. It carried 2,900 pounds of cargo and crew and had a 95-knot cruise speed. The HH-52 was an integral part of the testing that laid the foundation for nighttime helicopter search and rescue. The HU-16 proved to be a workhorse for the Coast Guard for decades. It holds nine world records for amphibious speed, altitude, and endurance. (U.S. Coast Guard.)

The HU-16 Albatross performs a JATO—or Jet Assisted Takeoff—after rendering assistance to the fishing vessel seen in the left-hand side of the picture. (U.S. Coast Guard.)

An HU-16 Albatross arrives on scene to render assistance to this sailing vessel in distress. For rescues outside of the HH-52A's range, the Albatross, or Goat as it was sometimes called, would land on the water to pick up the survivors. (U.S. Coast Guard.)

This is a view from the pilot's perspective looking back into the cabin of the HU-16 after picking up numerous survivors. (U.S. Coast Guard.)

A HO-4S performed an emergency landing at Grapevine Landing, North Carolina, on January 28, 1963. Another HO-4S brought the supplies and personnel required to complete the repairs, ensuring that the helicopter promptly returned to service. (U.S. Coast Guard.)

In 1962, a vicious northeaster hit the East Coast. Especially hard hit was Dare County, where steadily blowing hurricane-force winds caused the Atlantic Ocean to break through its bounds and spill over into inland areas. (U.S. Coast Guard.)

A HO-4S patrols the Outer Banks of North Carolina, surveying the damage-stricken coast and searching for people still in distress after the northeaster in 1962. (U.S. Coast Guard.)

On January 4, 1962, a U.S. Coast Guard HO-4S based in Elizabeth City approaches the trawler *Voyager* to deliver auxiliary pumps after the 70-foot trawler was reported taking on water 20 miles northeast of Currituck. (U.S. Coast Guard.)

AD3 (Aviation Machinist Mate, Third Class) Olen L. Elliot is congratulated by the pilots of an HU-16 Albatross for spotting a missing seaman who had jumped from the SS *Chemical Transporter*. Elliot was the aft watch on board when he sighted the man, who had been in the water for 15 hours. Lt. (jg) Art Foster, pilot (left), congratulates Elliot (center) as Lt. Frank Carman, co-pilot (right), watches. (U.S. Coast Guard.)

Aircrews conduct routine maintenance on a HU-16E Albatross inside the hangar.

The Coast Guard first evaluated the Convair C-131 in 1958 when it borrowed two aircraft from the navy. The C-131 can be seen here flying over northeast North Carolina in the early 1960s during one of these test flights. However, it was not until 1976 that the first C-131 was acquired from the Air Force and modified at AR&SC in Elizabeth City for further dissemination into the fleet. (U.S. Coast Guard.)

The flight line in the mid-1960s showcases the aircraft in the Air Station inventory. There are three HH-52s, three HU-16s, and eight C-130s. Some of the C-130s were in Elizabeth City because of a hurricane evacuation. If you look closely, the second C-130 on the top left has the current Coast Guard markings with the racing stripe, while the other C-130s have the older markings. (U.S. Coast Guard.)

A HU-16 is parked near the Air Station fire truck in the early 1960s, prior to the construction of the fire house. (James Doughty)

This is a close-up of a HO-4S parked on the flight line in front of Hanger 49. (James Doughty.)

A HO-4S hovers just off the deck in Portsmouth. Air Station Elizabeth City's area of operations includes the major harbors of Norfolk, Portsmouth, and Newport News, Virginia, as well as Morehead City and Wilmington, North Carolina. (U.S. Coast Guard.)

On September 13, 1960, CG1339, a C-130B (pictured above and below), taxis back onto the Coast Guard ramp after setting a record non-stop flight of 5,225 nautical miles. Air Station personnel are mustered in front of Hanger 49, rendering honors to the aircrew for setting this record. (U.S. Coast Guard.)

The commanding officer shakes hands with the pilot of CG1339, Lt. Comdr. Lloyd Kent, after his record flight that took 14 hours and 6 minutes. (U.S. Coast Guard.)

The crew poses for a photograph in front of the tail of CG1339 to document this record-setting flight. The aircrew consisted of the following personnel, from left to right: (first row) ADC (Aviation Machinist Mate Chief) H. Price, AD3 G. Koney, AD3 B. McDowell, AD3 M. Cobane, and PR1 (Public Relations First Class) G. Altenberger; (second row) Lt. Bruce Dewing (navigator), Lt. Comdr. Lloyd Kent (pilot), Comdr. Glen Thompson (co-pilot), AD1 (Aviation Machinist Mate First Class) R. Garvin, and AO1 (Aviation Ordinanceman First Class) W. Payne. (U.S. Coast Guard.)

Here is a picture of the "A" School's static trainer flight line in 1968. This ramp is now home to the Aviation Technical Training Center, where Coast Guard enlisted members come to earn their aviation rating. The training center was moved to Elizabeth City in the 1970s from Memphis, Tennessee. (U.S. Coast Guard.)

The Gaither family is escorted after being rescued by Lt. Gene Cooper. The Gaithers were friends with many of the pilots. Their boat *Playmate* hit a submerged object in the afternoon on June 10, 1962, on Albemarle Sound. The Gaithers spent the night clinging to the stricken vessel. Mr. Gaither swam to shore the next day to get help despite a broken collarbone. The first HO-4S helicopter, piloted by Lieutenant Conner, picked up Mr. Gaither to help search for his family. Lieutenant Cooper was on the second HO-4S helicopter after plotting his best guess location, and he flew the Weeksville NDB (omni-directional beacon) bearing right to the survivors. When Lieutenant Cooper's helicopter arrived on scene, only two feet of the bow was showing, and the mother had tied her two daughters to the boat so she could pull them back onboard when they were washed off by the rough seas. (U.S. Coast Guard.)

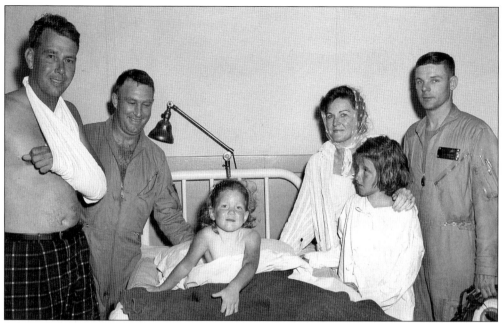

A happy Gaither family re-unites at the Coast Guard Air Station Dispensary in Elizabeth City, after a harrowing experience left them clinging to the wreckage of their boat, *Playmate*. Smiles of relief from the father, mother, and their daughters are mustered for Lt. Richard Conner, the pilot who picked up Mr. Gaither on the beach, and for Lt. Gene Cooper, the pilot who pulled Mrs. Gaither and her daughters to safety. (U.S. Coast Guard.)

This March 1963 picture shows the entrance to the infirmary, which now is home to a marine safety detachment. The infirmary has been replaced by a state-of-the-art clinic that supports all of the other commands on the entire Elizabeth City complex and falls under the Support Centers command. (U.S. Coast Guard.)

A H-52 flies over the countryside surrounding Air Station Elizabeth City during its introduction in 1961. As the first Coast Guard helicopter powered by a gas turbine engine, the H-52 proved to be extremely reliable, in part because a governor prevented the engine from ever having to operate at 100 percent. (U.S. Coast Guard.)

A H-52 slowly descends for a water landing. The boarding platform extends just behind the right main landing gear. (U.S. Coast Guard.)

The HH-52's amphibious ability enabled it to respond in many different ways to emergencies at sea. Here the HH-52 is pictured landing on the water. The Sea Guard holds the record for most lives saved over the operational career of a helicopter. (U.S. Coast Guard.)

This HH-52 Sea Guard shows off another one of its attractive traits, being towed after a mechanical failure. Note the inflation bags on the left and right sponsons and the tow line off the nose of the aircraft. By the early 1970s, the Coast Guard had an entire inventory of rotary-winged aircraft that could float. This is a great characteristic to have in case of engine failure over the water while doing a rescue. (U.S. Coast Guard.)

A HH-52 crew practices recovering personnel from the water. The flight mechanic can be seen kneeling on the platform, helping another crewman back into the aircraft. The metal grate platform extends out into the water, making deployment and recovery of personnel from the water very easy. (U.S. Coast Guard.)

Personnel from the fishing trawler *Oriental* are rescued after their vessel ran aground in heavy seas on the Outer Banks of North Carolina. Here the first of three survivors are hoisted clear of the vessel by a HH-52 Sea Guard based in Elizabeth City. (U.S. Coast Guard.)

The second of three survivors is hoisted from the fishing vessel *Oriental* after the ship ran aground. Despite the tall masts and fishing gear rigged above the deck, both men were recovered without incident. The *Oriental* reportedly served as Adolf Hitler's yacht. (U.S. Coast Guard.)

Maintenance crews are working on a C-123B. The engine cowling can be seen folded back to reveal the large, 2,300-horsepower, Pratt and Whitney R-2800-99W Double Wasp, 18-cylinder, radial-piston engine. (U.S. Coast Guard.)

A C-123B sits on the Coast Guard ramp in Elizabeth City. A Coast Guard DC-3 (R-4D) can be seen in the background. (U.S. Coast Guard.)

A HU-16E Albatross with the new (in 1966) paint scheme is parked on the ramp opposite a C-123 in the old livery. From this location, amphibious aircraft could start engines on land, taxi into the water to conduct water operations, and then taxi back onto land. In the background are several Coast Guard aircraft, including a C-123B, a HO-4S, two additional HU-16Es, and a PBY-5A. (U.S. Coast Guard.)

A HU-16E displays its new paint job. The original design of the Coast Guard shield can be seen overlaying the stripe. Eventually, the outline of the shield and the motto were removed, leaving only the Coast Guard symbol with crossed anchors. (U.S. Coast Guard.)

This is an aerial photograph of the Coast Guard Air Station as it appeared in 1964. Runway 07/25 was the primary strip used by the field at the time. Runway 10/28 underwent a major rehabilitation between 1965 and 1967 and remains the main runway at the airport. (U.S. Coast Guard.)

A HU-16 begins overhaul at Aircraft Repair and Supply Center in the early 1960s. The HU-16 is shown with the original paint scheme, while the C-123B was intentionally left unpainted. (U.S. Coast Guard.)

Shown here is a depot-level overhaul at AR&SC in the mid-1960s. In the foreground, the tail section has been removed from an HU-16E, while three H-52s and two HO-4Ss undergo varying degrees of maintenance in the background. (U.S. Coast Guard.)

Pictured here is an HU-16E undergoing a major overhaul. The aircraft paint has been stripped, and the tail section, propellers, and landing gear have all been removed for inspection. (U.S. Coast Guard.)

Three HU-16E Albatrosses are seen going through various stages of overhaul. (U.S. Coast Guard.)

A HU-16's landing gear gets a final inspection after going through overhaul. The original paint scheme is depicted. (U.S. Coast Guard.)

The AR&SC team responsible for servicing CG1394 H-52 is shown standing in front of the aircraft, which was the 100th H-52A to be overhauled at the facility. (U.S. Coast Guard.)

A Coast Guard H-3 is shown coming in for a water landing at Air Station Elizabeth City. A corner of the launch ramp can be seen in the foreground. (U.S. Coast Guard.)

This is an H-3 taxiing after completing a water landing. The H-3 was the last amphibious helicopter to be used by the Coast Guard. (U.S. Coast Guard.)

USCGC *Eagle*, America's tall ship, needed the Air Station's help in the early 1970s, and a HH-3F Pelican flew out to conduct a medical evacuation off the North Carolina coast. (U.S. Coast Guard.)

The HH-3F conducts the medivac hoist from the *Eagle*'s motor launch. With 143-foot masts, it was too dangerous to hoist directly from the tall ship. (U.S. Coast Guard.)

This H-3 conducts a rescue in rough seas off a merchant ship. To assist in the evacuation from a disabled vessel, a basket is often lowered to hoist survivors into the aircraft. (U.S. Coast Guard.)

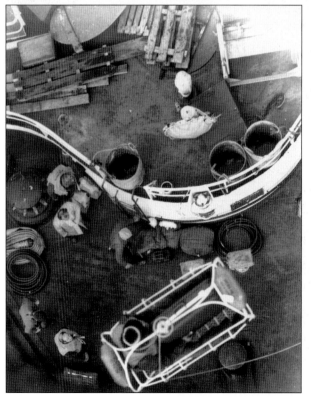

This is the helicopter basket on deck during a rescue. The personnel on deck had many hazards to overcome in order to carry out a successful rescue. In addition to the movement of the vessel they were on, the deck personnel also must deal with the high winds and noise of the helicopter and the static charge that is built up by the rotor system. Unaware individuals can receive a nasty electrical shock if they are not careful. (U.S. Coast Guard.)

For those who are immobile or have a potential spinal injury, a litter is used to hoist them to safety. Here a H-3 uses a litter to airlift a survivor into the aircraft. (U.S. Coast Guard.)

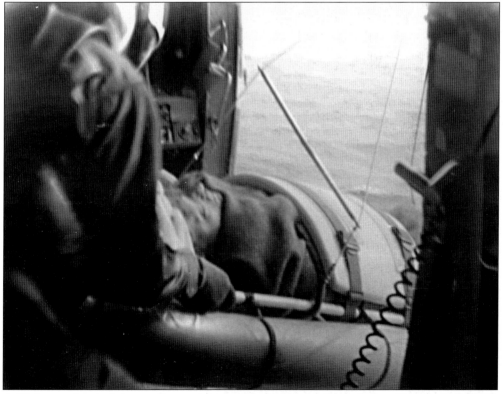

A flight mechanic brings a litter with an injured person through the side of a H-3. (U.S. Coast Guard.)

Capt. William H. Brinkmeyer is welcomed to Air Station Elizabeth City with a traditional "wetting-down" after the pilots and crew learned he had recently been promoted. The top part of the picture shows the captain in flight just prior to impact. The bottom of the picture shows the watery aftermath. (U.S. Coast Guard.)

The Coast Guard has been an active participant in every major United States military operation since its conception. This crew from Elizabeth City flew 42 missions in Vietnam from November 1966 to January 1967. (U.S. Coast Guard.)

A H-52 makes an approach to the stern of a merchant vessel. The Coast Guard is frequently involved in the emergency medical evacuation (medivac) of injured crew people from vessels at sea. (U.S. Coast Guard.)

A H-52 responds to a request for a medivac and deploys a basket to the stern of a merchant vessel to retrieve the injured crewman. (U.S. Coast Guard.)

This is a navy P-2V on the ramp of the Air Station. The tail code indicates it is from NAS Willow Grove. (U.S. Coast Guard.)

A PT-22 manufactured by Ryan Aircraft Corporation is parked on the Coast Guard ramp in Elizabeth City, where it was stored for several months. The airplane was owned by an ensign stationed at the Air Station, who flew in with it upon completion of flight training. (James E. Mahoney.)

CG1414 is parked in front of the Elizabeth City hangar and tower. This was the only C-130 E-model the Coast Guard ever operated. Note the vandalism on the auxiliary fuel tank from our U.S. Navy brethren. (James E. Mahoney.)

The Air Station is shown here as it appeared in 1967. A C-130 Hercules and HU-16 Albatross are parked on the ramp, while a H-52 Sea Guard can be seen just inside the hangar. (James E. Mahoney.)

This HH-52 Sea Guard is parked on the ramp in Elizabeth City, probably during a phased maintenance at the Aircraft Repair and Supply Center. The predominantly orange paint scheme was used primarily by those aircraft deploying on the back of icebreakers bound for Antarctica to the south or the frozen north of the Artic. (James E. Mahoney.)

Looking from the Boat House, the main hangar with control tower can be seen, with the administration building in the foreground as it appeared in 1971. On the far right you can just make out the corner of the Parachute Loft and Survival Equipment Building. (James I. Doughty.)

Looking north from the control tower in 1971, the Parachute Loft and Survival Equipment Building can be seen. On the far right is the infirmary, followed by the Base Officers' Quarters and officers' mess behind that, and beyond that is the peaked roof of the swimming pool building. (James I. Doughty.)

Air Station personnel take a break on a hot summer day in 1971 to play a game of volleyball on the ramp. In the hangar, a HU-16E Albatross is prepped and ready for routine maintenance. In the background are two HC-130 Hercules, a HU-16E Albatross, a HH-52 Sea Guard, and, on the far left, the "Round House" barracks building. (James I. Doughty.)

In this view, taken from behind the Boat House on the Pasquotank River in June 1971, the AR&SC building can be seen on the left, with the large round barracks building pictured on the right. (James I. Doughty.)

This is a view at the Pasquotank River and Boat House as seen from the tower in 1971. The old exchange building is on the left. (James I. Doughty.)

Coast Guard members take a break for lunch at the "snack shack" behind the children's swimming pool building in 1971. (James I. Doughty.)

This is how the Air Station looked in 1967. The foreground shows a close-up of some the AR&SC supply warehouse and the area where Thrun Hall Enlisted Barracks, the "Round House," would be built. (U.S. Coast Guard.)

This aerial shot of the Air Station and Aircraft Repair and Supply Center (AR&SC) was taken around 1967. You can see the AR&SC facility in the foreground with the Air Station position just beyond that. The building on the far left in the background is the Training Center. Thrun Hall Enlisted Barracks, "The Round House" located between AR&SC and the Air Station, had not been built yet. (U.S. Coast Guard.)

Here is the air traffic control tower in 1973. Beyond the tower you can see three C-130s and a U.S. Navy H-53 Sea Stallion parked on the ramp. (U.S. Coast Guard.)

Three

TRANSITION AND GROWTH
1976–1990

Maggi Cathey took this picture of her husband, Lt. Bob Cathey, taxiing for takeoff. You can see the condensation formed by the propeller blades as the aircraft proceeds down the field. (Maggi Cathey.)

The most welcome sight in the world for many mariners is a H-3 Pelican hovering in with rescue basket ready for immediate pickup. The boat hull of the H-3 that allowed the helicopter to land, float, and even taxi in the water is readily apparent in this shot. (U.S. Coast Guard.)

This circular rotor wash was made by a H-3 while conducting rescue hoisting operations. The H-3's five-bladed rotor system made for a relatively manageable rotor wash pattern that allowed both pilot and flight mechanic to stay very low to the water and affect a rapid rescue of survivors without the possibility of drowning them. The H-3 is thought of by many who flew it as the perfect SAR platform. (U.S. Coast Guard.)

A HH-52 Sea Guard approaches the stern of a sinking merchant vessel. A life raft full of survivors can be seen drifting between the helicopter and the wreck. (U.S. Coast Guard.)

A C-130 equipped with Jet Assisted Takeoff (JATO) practices short field operations. The Coast Guard frequently pre-stationed JATO packs on short fields, generally in New England or Canada, in the event that a C-130 was required to land there as a result of reaching "Bingo," or critical fuel levels. This gave the C-130s greater flexibility in responding to SAR cases and extended the amount of time they could remain on the scene. (U.S. Coast Guard.)

In addition to accelerating the aircraft much more quickly, the JATO packs also increased the angle at which the aircraft could climb out. Despite their effectiveness, they were rarely used except for training, and eventually all JATO mounts were removed from the C-130s in the Coast Guard inventory. (U.S. Coast Guard.)

This is a view of the present-day Support Center building from the banks of the Pasquotank River in the late 1970s. The base's tennis courts are in view on the right side of the picture. By the 1990s, the tennis courts had become parking lots to accommodate the growth of the complex's commands. (U.S. Coast Guard.)

Comdr. Jay Taylor took this picture of the Air Station in 1979 while flying in the co-pilot seat of a HH-3. Another HH-3 can be seen on the Air Station's ramp, while a C-130 conducts engine run-ups on the taxiway. (Jay Taylor.)

The Coast Guard Air Station has always been a significant part of the local community. Here, a group of kindergarteners from Elizabeth City pose in front of a H-3 Pelican with Lt. Jay Taylor and Lt. Roger Whorton. (Jay Taylor.)

An Elizabeth City HH-52 Sea Guard is shown landing in the vicinity of an environmental response exercise for the National Strike Force (NSF). The mid-1970s saw a general awakening of the nation's consciousness to the hazards and threats posed by industrial pollution and accidents. The Coast Guard was at the forefront of this expansion of capability with the creation of the NSF, based in Elizabeth City. This unit is responsible for providing on-scene expertise to the federal incident commander for environmental events of national significance. Air Station Elizabeth City is responsible for providing logistics support to the NSF during spills of national significance. (U.S. Coast Guard.)

Lt. Jay Taylor practices hoisting a litter from small boat No. 40555 from Elizabeth City. Helicopter crews continue to practice hoisting evolutions in order to fine tune the skills necessary to respond to a SAR case. (Jay Taylor.)

A helicopter crewman is hoisted into a H-3 from the Air Station's aviation training boat (ATB). The ATB was maintained and staffed by Air Station personnel to support the training needs of the pilots and crew. (Jay Taylor)

CG1437 practices rescue hoisting to the Air Station's ATB in 1978. One of the harder hoisting evolutions was the dead in the water, or DIW, rescue hoist. The challenge to the pilot and flight mechanic was steering the helicopter in a manner to not spin the vessel through the wind. (Jay Taylor.)

A flight mechanic and trainee prepare to begin hoisting operations from the door of a H-3. Another of the numerous advantages of the Sikorsky helicopter was its stand-up cabin, which allowed the hoist operators room to stand while they operated the hoist and all of the associated rescue equipment. (U.S. Coast Guard.)

CG1437 hovers low over a vessel prior to sending the training litter out the door for an underway hoist. Of the various rescue devices the Coast Guard uses to rescue survivors, the rescue litter presents a greater challenge to the flight mechanic operating the hoist because of its larger size and bulk. (Jay Taylor.)

This is an excellent picture of an Air Station Elizabeth City H-3 carrying out a medical evacuation to one of the many charter fishing boats that still operate off the Outer Banks of North Carolina. The rescue litter and trail line used to stabilize it on its trip to and from the vessel are visible in the center of the picture. (U.S. Coast Guard.)

The late 1970s and early 1980s were the heyday for the amateur drug runner. It was also the heyday for almost all Coast Guard units, as they reacquainted themselves with the lost art of contraband enforcement, not used since Prohibition. Here an Air Station Elizabeth City helicopter crew celebrates the healthy seizure of six bales of marijuana off the Outer Banks of the Carolinas. (U.S. Coast Guard.)

This H-3 will live to fly another day. A Sikorsky Skycrane hovers over an Air Station Elizabeth City H-3 that experienced an engine failure and had to land in the water off the coast of Virginia in 1978. The amphibious capability of the Pelican paid large dividends during its 25-year career, not only in lives but dollars saved in many situations similar to this. (U.S. Coast Guard.)

The H-3 is lifted fully out of the water and begins its transport back to Elizabeth City for repair. The Skycrane was a U.S. Army helicopter that was based in Fort Eustis, Virginia. The Skycrane had the ability to lift 47,000 pounds and could be flown facing forward in the standard cockpit or facing aft in a cupola that allowed the pilot to see the load he was hoisting. (U.S. Coast Guard.)

Santa gets hoisted for Christmas in the Air Station's holiday card from 1977. The reindeer were saved and lived to fly another day. (Air Station Elizabeth City Administration Department.)

Comdr. Frank Olsen, executive officer for the Air Station, demonstrates the proper technique for refueling the H-3 in 1979. Individuals refueling the H-3 had to stand with their arms outstretched to ensure the fuel would not roll into the tank and then back out of the overflow pipe to douse them. Commander Olsen unfortunately was killed in a H-52 crash while he was commanding officer of Air Station Port Angeles. (Jay Taylor.)

The new buildings of the Aviation Technical Training Center (ATTC) are shown looking south from over the approach end of runway 19 around 1981. Three HU-16s and one C-131 used for hands-on training of the "A" School students are visible in the center foreground. The 1970s–1980s were another period of growth for the Elizabeth City complex, as Coast Guard aviation continued moving toward the future. (U.S. Coast Guard.)

An overhead close-up of ATTC shows the classroom building in the center of the picture. The light-colored roof section in the center left portion of the picture is part of the hands-on laboratory portion of the school. The nose of one of the HU-16s used for AD/AM (Aviation Machinist Mate/Aviation Structural Mechanic) training is in the extreme left side of the picture. Also note that the hangar that was present in the previous picture is no longer. (U.S. Coast Guard.)

A HH-52 Sea Guard lifts into a hover over Golf Taxiway for a functional check flight following depot maintenance from the Aircraft Repair and Supply Center. Following each depot maintenance period, the helicopters had to be flown to ensure all flight, mechanical, and mission systems operated correctly. This process often took a week or more. (U.S. Coast Guard.)

A petty officer works on the rotor head of a HH-52 at AR&SC in Hangar 78 in early 1982. (U.S. Coast Guard.)

A C-130 crew prepares for a flight by briefing all anticipated evolutions beforehand. The picture is taken from the back of the cargo compartment looking forward toward the nose of the aircraft. The flight deck is not visible from the cargo compartment because of the avionics rack. (U.S. Coast Guard.)

Two crew members are welcomed back to Elizabeth City after completing a flight. (U.S. Coast Guard.)

C-131 and C-130 static displays sit in front of Thrun Hall during an air show in 1983. Thousands of people from all over northeastern North Carolina and southeastern Virginia were able to visit the base and view flight and static demonstrations. (U.S. Coast Guard.)

Two survivors set off a signal flare during the 1983 air show at the beginning of the Coast Guard's rescue demonstration. (U.S. Coast Guard.)

A Pelican lands in the river to show off its amphibious capability. The H-3 was able to rescue many people by just landing next to the survivor and pulling them into the cabin. (U.S. Coast Guard.)

An HH-3E Jolly Green Giant, the U.S. Air Force's version of the Sikorsky rescue helicopter, sits on the Air Station ramp. The rescue equipment used by the Jolly Green Giant was specific to the mission of combat search and rescue, and the Jolly Green Giant was not amphibious. (U.S. Coast Guard.)

A horse of a different color, the U.S. Coast Guard version of the H-3 sits farther down the flight line from the U.S. Air Force Jolly Green Giant. The open engine bays and rescue hoist on the right side of the aircraft are readily apparent as visitors climb up the helicopter entry door. (U.S. Coast Guard.)

An 82-foot Point-class cutter is tied up at the Elizabeth City Base boat ramp during the air show. The presence of a Coast Guard cutter in this part of the Pasquotank River was rare because of the shallow water of the river and the navigational draft of the 82-foot boat. The Point-class cutters were more comfortable working the areas five to 50 miles offshore, conducting law enforcement and SAR missions. (U.S. Coast Guard.)

This is the static-display flight line during the 1983 air show. From left to right, a H-52, H-3, HU-25, and C-131 give the American taxpayer a look at the first team of Search and Rescue during the early 1980s. (U.S. Coast Guard.)

Navy SEALs from the Amphibious Base Little Creek, Virginia, give a land parachuting demonstration. Heavy lift helicopters from Fort Bragg, North Carolina, and Norfolk, Virginia, are visible in the foreground. (U.S. Coast Guard.)

The Little Creek–based SEALs moved their demo to the river to give the public an idea of their marine capabilities. (U.S. Coast Guard.)

Sailing vessels look on as the last of the airborne SEALs complete their parachute demonstration with a watery landing. (U.S. Coast Guard.)

A Coast Guard C-130 crew from Elizabeth City pauses for a picture prior to their flight. Every year since at least 1923 a wreath is dedicated and dropped at the site where the HMS *Titanic* sank on April 15, 1912. The International Ice Patrol was formed as a direct result of the events that transpired on the evening of April 14 and the subsequent morning. (U.S. Coast Guard.)

A drop crew prepares to jettison a marker buoy out the back of a C-130. Since its inception, the International Ice Patrol has continued to take advantage of new technology. This includes aircraft that replaced ships as the primary means of detection; the development and application of radar to locate the icebergs; and the practice of dropping newer and more sophisticated buoys to help track icebergs, water temperatures, and currents. (U.S. Coast Guard.)

A crew poses for a picture on the ramp in front of their C-130 after an international ice patrol. While icebergs typically are found in the summer months, the ice patrol season usually starts in February and runs through late July. (U.S. Coast Guard.)

PO Gerry Watts graduates from aviation electricians' "A" School. The Missouri native would go on to reach the rank of chief warrant officer in a career that included service on HU-25 Falcons, H-3s, and H-60s. (Gerry Watts.)

Here is Hangar 49 on a late afternoon in the summer of 1983. The aircraft ramp was completely open to passing traffic, and the Thrun Hall enlisted barracks parking lot is in the foreground. (U.S. Coast Guard.)

Despite their incredible durability and effectiveness, even C-130s must eventually be retired. Here CG1454 is pictured at Davis-Monthan Air Force Base after it was retired. Low-altitude operations over the ocean contribute to corrosion and the formation of microscopic cracks over time. Eventually, the aircraft must be repaired or sent to the "bone-yard" and replaced. Today, Elizabeth City is host to the C-130 J Program, whose mission is to prepare the next-generation C-130 for service in the Coast Guard. (U.S. Coast Guard.)

A C-131 sits tied down to the ramp area on the northwest side of the air base complex in 1985. By this time, the C-131, which was an interim solution for the service's needs for a medium-range, fixed-wing SAR aircraft, had been retired in lieu of the HU-25 Guardian. This aircraft eventually became a fire trainer for the airport fire department. (U.S. Coast Guard.)

The Air Station's 32-foot Aviation Training Boat (ATB) supports hoisting operations with an H-3. By the early 1980s, the 40-foot ATB had been superseded by the smaller, more economical 32-foot boat. The Air Station's personnel were still responsible for operating and maintaining the vessel, but it provided an excellent training platform for "homegrown" training for the Air Station's helicopter crews. (Gerry Watts.)

The Air Station buildings are being added to in this picture from 1985. Hangar 55 is under construction; this hangar would allow indoor parking for two of the long-range SAR aircraft. The airport fire department buildings have also been completed and are seen at the center right of the picture, just below a U.S. Air Force F-15 Eagle that has landed with an in-flight emergency. (U.S. Coast Guard.)

CG1712 taxis for takeoff in front of Thrun Hall enlisted barracks and Hangar 49 in this picture from March 1989. (U.S. Coast Guard.)

CG02 approaches for landing at Elizabeth City. The Gulfstream VC-4, a civilian G-I, was temporarily stationed at AR&SC in the late 1980s, a period of thin budgets for the U.S. Coast Guard, during which it handled logistics and administrative flying for the depot. (U.S. Coast Guard.)

A U.S. Coast Guard E-2 Hawkeye from the Coast Guard Aviation Detachment in Norfolk, Virginia, turns on the Elizabeth City ramp in 1988. The Coast Guard started a program that utilized the Airborne Early Warning aircraft to coordinate the service's counter-narcotics operations in the Caribbean and Gulf of Mexico. The program was ended following the tragic crash of one of the aircraft in Roosevelt Roads, Puerto Rico. (U.S. Coast Guard.)

Shown here is the Air Station ramp in 1989. The HH-3 and HC-130 were the stalwarts of Coast

Guard aviation for long-range SAR during the 1970s and 1980s. (U.S. Coast Guard.)

This is the front of a C-130 Hercules parked on the Air Station ramp in front of the base's barracks, otherwise known as the "Round House." (U.S. Coast Guard.)

A H-3 flies in formation with a 1300-series C-130. The task of helicopter escort required the Hercules to maintain station with the helicopter to ensure coverage in the event of an in-flight emergency. One of the techniques for providing station coverage is the formation flight. (U.S. Coast Guard.)

Four

OLD GUARD TO NEW
1991–2005

CG1483 sits in front of one of the first H-60s the Coast Guard owned in 1991. Elizabeth City was the first operational unit to receive H-60s, because it was designated the H-60 prime unit, which is tasked with prototyping new equipment and maintenance procedures for the H-60. (AMTC [Aviation Maintenance Technician Chief] Wes Fleming.)

On July 3, 1991, a Sikorsky representative addresses the Air Station at the HH-60J dedication ceremony. The HH-60J replaced the HH-3F as the Coast Guard's medium-range helicopter, and Air Station Elizabeth City was the first to get the H-60. (U.S. Coast Guard.)

This is the HH-60J dedication ceremony on July 3, 1991, with an HH-3F in the background. (U.S. Coast Guard.)

An Air Station crew member paddles his "boat" in the annual Anything Floats but a Boat Race in the Pasquotank River. This race involves the various departments at the Air Station constructing a boat out of materials that normally would not be used for a boat. This long-standing tradition in Elizabeth City has proven to be a memorable event for participants. (U.S. Coast Guard.)

The so-called boats line up for the start of the Anything Floats but a Boat Race. (U.S. Coast Guard.)

Lt. (jg) Tony Clark is interviewed by the media after pulling four individuals from the grasp of the Atlantic Ocean. (U.S. Coast Guard.)

A Schweizer RG-8 powered glider sits on the Aviation Repair and Supply Center's ramp. The RG-8 was used for counter-narcotics surveillance in the 7th District during the 1980s. The supply warehouse and the enlisted barracks, known as Thrun Hall or the "Round House," are on the right. (U.S. Coast Guard.)

The survivors that Lt. (jg) Tony Clark rescued talk with Capt. Terry Beacham, the Air Station's commanding officer, after their rescue from the Atlantic Ocean. (U.S. Coast Guard.)

The air station is frequently asked to perform SAR demonstrations at air shows in the local area. This photograph shows a simulated survivor and rescue swimmer being brought into a helicopter by the flight mechanic during the Andrews Air Force Base Joint Services Open House in 1991. (CWO Michael Proctor.)

You can see the thousands of people that made up the audience for this demonstration at Andrews Air Force Base in Washington, D.C. (CWO Michael Proctor.)

This rescue swimmer, ASM2 (Aviation Survivalman Second Class) Scott Adlen, conducts an inspection of the tail prior to conducting sling load operations on Bodie Island in the Outer Banks to remove an aid to a navigation buoy. (AMTC Wes Fleming.)

A HH-60J makes an approach to the beach on Bodie Island in the Outer Banks in 1994 to remove an aid to navigation buoy. The ground crew is AD3 Tim Craft. (AMTC Wes Fleming.)

The buoy is picked up on Bodie Island using the cargo hook of the H-60. The H-60's cargo hook is rated to lift 6,000 pounds. (AMTC Wes Fleming.)

The H-60 successfully lifts the buoy and flies away to transport it. (ATMC Wes Fleming.)

The sailboat *Marine Flower II* was in transit to the Bahamas when it was caught between Hurricane Gordon and a northeaster. A H-60 from Elizabeth City was sent over 400 nautical miles offshore to rescue a family of four, which included the father, mother, 13-year-old daughter, and a four-month-old infant. The aircrew consisted of Dave Gundersen (pilot), Dan Molthen (co-pilot), Bobby Blackwell (flight mechanic), and Mario Vittone (rescue swimmer). The father had single-handedly piloted the boat for 44 consecutive hours when he determined that they needed help. Upon arriving on scene, Vittone was lowered into the 20-foot seas and was unable to reach the vessel due to the horrific on-scene conditions. A second attempt was made, bringing Vittone 15 feet from the vessel when a wave washed over the mother and four-month-old infant. He quickly grasped the mother and child, keeping both their heads above the water and safely getting them aboard the helicopter. (Mario Vittone.)

Here is a view from the helicopter looking at the superstructure of the USS *America* as the rescue helicopter received fuel in order to execute the rescue of the *Marine Flower II*. Due to Hurricane Gordon and the vast distance needing to be traveled, the H-60 took on fuel heading out to the rescue and while returning. The landing on the boat was also complicated by 20- to 30-foot seas, but Dan Molthen safely made both landings. (Mario Vittone.)

The aircrew from the rescue of the sailboat *Mirage* poses for a picture in 1995 in front of a H-60. Once the helicopter arrived on scene, 265 nautical miles from Wilmington, North Carolina, three individuals jumped in the water. The rescue swimmer, PO Mike Odhom, got all three survivors into the helicopter when the cable on the hoist frayed. With no way to recover the rescue swimmer and low on fuel, the helicopter had to depart the scene. A C-130 stayed overhead of Petty Officer Odhom until another helicopter was able to rescue him, but Petty Officer Odhom still spent five and a half hours in the Atlantic Ocean. Due to this case, the Coast Guard developed the emergency recovery device (ERD). The air crew, from left to right, are Mark Bafetti (flight mechanic), Mike Odom (rescue swimmer), Mario Vittone (rescue swimmer), Joseph Balda (pilot), and Guy Pearce (co-pilot). (U.S. Coast Guard.)

Lt. Rob Kortus stands at attention while being awarded an air medal by his commanding officer for the rescue of six people off of the sailboat *Night Sound* 435 nautical miles east of Norfolk, Virginia. (U.S. Coast Guard.)

The flight mechanic conducts a safety inspection, holding onto the swimmer while the helicopter moves into position. (U.S. Coast Guard.)

The flight mechanic prepares the rescue basket so that it can be lowered and used to recover survivors or the swimmer. (U.S. Coast Guard.)

The flight mechanic grasps the rescue basket and pulls the rescue swimmer back into the helicopter during training exercises. (U.S. Coast Guard.)

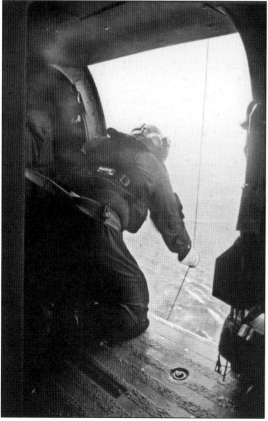

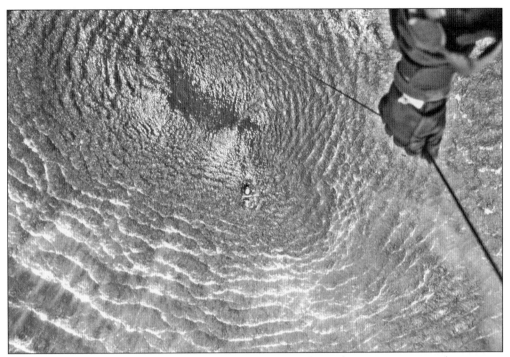

The flight mechanic, who is responsible for providing the pilot with conning commands, positions the helicopter so that the rescue swimmer can reach the hook on the hoist cable and connect it to his harness. While the flight mechanic manages the hoist cable, the rescue swimmer prepares the survivor for the ride up to the helicopter. (U.S. Coast Guard.)

Lieutenant Colonel St. Germain of the Canadian Air Force and Captain Walz, commanding officer of Air Station Elizabeth City, exchange plaques as sister squadrons. (U.S. Coast Guard.)

The sister squadron team poses in front of a Canadian C-130. (U.S. Coast Guard.)

Here is a C-130 in a blizzard in Saint Johns, Newfoundland, during an International Ice Patrol mission. (U.S. Coast Guard.)

CG1503 sits on the ramp prior to an International Ice Patrol mission. The external power cart can be seen just forward of the nose, which provides power to the aircraft while the crew conducts its preflight checks. (U.S. Coast Guard.)

A C-130 is pulled into the hangar in Saint Johns, Newfoundland, after an ice patrol mission, to keep ice from building up on the airframe in an approaching storm. Snow can already be seen accumulating on the nose of the aircraft. (U.S. Coast Guard.)

A C-130 drop master is shown deploying a buoy for monitoring icebergs. International Ice Patrol personnel use several different systems to mark and track ice floes in the North Atlantic shipping lanes. (U.S. Coast Guard.)

C-130 crew members prepare equipment for deployment during an International Ice Patrol mission. All straps, latches, and fittings must be inspected to ensure a successful drop. (U.S. Coast Guard.)

A C-130 ice patrol crew gets ready for a drop. Once the crate is free from the aircraft, it will open, and a WOCE (World Ocean Circulation Experiment) buoy will be released. (U.S. Coast Guard.)

A WOCE buoy is deployed from the back of a C-130. The parachute can be seen in the center of the shot, just above the crewman's arm. A static line used to open the crate can be seen just above the crewman's head. (U.S. Coast Guard.)

A van is flooded out during Hurricane Floyd in Rocky Mount, North Carolina. The hurricane stalled just as it hit shore and dumped a lot of rain on the coastal areas. In this hurricane, the flooding that resulted from rain was more devastating than the wind. This resulted in Air Station Elizabeth City performing a lot of inland rescues. (U.S. Coast Guard.)

An Elizabeth City H-60 lands on U.S. Highway 64 to drop off survivors trapped by flooding due to Hurricane Floyd. (U.S. Coast Guard.)

Here is a young boy disembarking from a helicopter at the junction of U.S. Highway 64 and Interstate 95 in Rocky Mount, North Carolina, which was used as the landing zone for the rescue operations on September 17, 1999. (U.S. Coast Guard.)

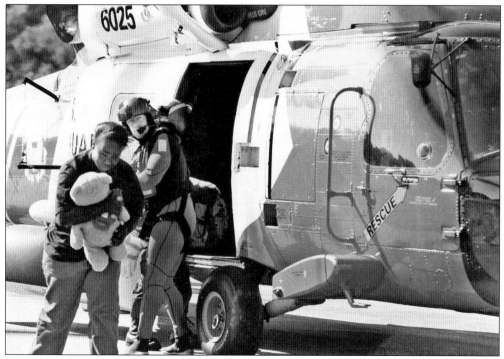

A young woman clutches her teddy bear, which was the only personal possession she was able to take before her home was consumed by the flood waters. (U.S. Coast Guard.)

Air Station personnel pose for a picture with Pres. Bill Clinton, Secretary of Transportation Rodney Slater, and Commandant of the Coast Guard Adm. James Loy. (U.S. Coast Guard.)

Air Station Elizabeth City musters on the ramp in 1999. The Air Station at the time was made up of crews and personnel to support three HH-60s and four C-130s. (U.S. Coast Guard.)

Members of the Tuskeegee Airmen visit the Coast Guard Air Station in Elizabeth City. (U.S. Coast Guard.)

On December 17, 2000, a Cost Guard HH-60 (CG6031) hoisted 26 survivors from the sinking *Sea Breeze*. This picture was taken by the co-pilot of the second helicopter to arrive on scene. If you look closely, the first helicopter can be seen just below the left row of life rafts. In the background, a C-130 (also out of Elizabeth City) provides a communications guard for the helicopters. (Steve Bonn.)

CG6031, a HH-60J Jayhawk, recovers its rescue swimmer, Darren Reeves, after hoisting 26 survivors aboard. Lt. Dan Molthen and Lt. (jg) Craig Neubecker were the pilot and co-pilot, respectively. The flight mechanic was AMT2 Loren Green. (Steve Bonn.)

CG6031 departs the sinking cruise ship *Sea Breeze*. The picture was taken from the second helicopter on scene, which proceeded to hoist the remaining eight survivors. (Steve Bonn.)

Captain Odom recognizes the aircrews that participated in the rescue of 39 crew members from the stricken cruise ship *Sea Breeze* in December 2000. One helicopter hoisted 26 crew members, setting a record for the number of people in the back of a HH-60J (a total of 28 people: 26 survivors plus two crew). (U.S. Coast Guard.)

Lt. (jg) Craig Neubecker can be seen standing next to a HH-60J from Elizabeth City after it landed at Aid to Navigation Station Chesapeake Bay Light. (Craig Neubecker.)

A Coast Guard C-130 can be seen flying in front of a giant iceberg floating in the North Atlantic. CG1500 is currently the oldest aircraft in the Coast Guard's inventory. (U.S. Coast Guard.)

A Coast Guard HH-60J, with a C-130 flying communications cover in the background, makes an approach to the cruise ship *Rotterdam* just prior to a medivac. (Craig Neubecker.)

The bow of the cruise ship *Rotterdam* is visible as a HH-60J makes its approach to deploy their rescue swimmer. A C-130 can be seen in the background providing communications support. (Craig Neubecker.)

A HH-60J responds to a medivac request from the cruise ship *Rotterdam*. The ship's nurse can be seen here being hoisted onboard in the helicopter's basket. Still on deck, the patient is being secured in the helicopter's litter. Lt. (jg) Craig Neubecker is in the right seat conducting the hoist, with Lt. Comdr. Paul Franklin in the left seat. (Craig Neubecker.)

In 2002, a rescue swimmer presents aircrew wings to a Robert McWilliams Honorary Rescue Swimmer. The boy was treated to a HH-60J flight and tour of the Air Station facilities as part of the Make-A-Wish Foundation. (U.S. Coast Guard.)

Coast Guard aircrew participates in the Make-A-Wish Foundation program, posing for a picture after their flight. (U.S. Coast Guard.)

Rear Adm. Sally Brice-O'Hara presents Lt. Frank Flood with the Coast Guard Commendation Medal for his role as the co-pilot during the rescue of 17 Russians from the merchant vessel *White Seal*. (U.S. Coast Guard.)

Elizabeth City sent a delegation to the grave of Comdr. Elmer Fowler "Archie" Stone, the first Coast Guard pilot, on Veteran's Day in 2001. Commander Stone was the pilot and navigator on the first trans-Atlantic flight. Pictured from left to right are CWO Mike Proctor, SCPO Kieth Reese, CPO Mustafa Bozkurt, and CWO Gerrald Watts. (Mike Proctor.)

Capt. Rod Ansley, commanding officer of Air Station Elizabeth City from 2003 to 2005 (center, in white shirt), ensures his C-130 and HH-60 ready crews are prepared for the day's missions. In addition to managing the traditional SAR and law-enforcement missions most common to an air station, Captain Ansley was responsible for coordinating the Air Station's integration and increased operations associated with homeland security. (U.S. Coast Guard.)

A C-130 arrives on the scene of a cruise ship with a patient in need of a medivac. For cases that are farther off shore, a C-130 will often accompany, or precede, a HH-60 helicopter to help provide communications support. If the C-130 arrives on scene first, they may help prepare the ship by giving the ship heading instructions or briefing the ship's crew members on what will be expected of them during the hoisting evolution. (U.S. Coast Guard.)

Passengers on board the cruise ship gather as the HH-60 makes its approach to the vessel. The flight mechanic's head can be seen leaning out the side of the helicopter as he gives continual reports to the pilot on the relative position of the aircraft to the cruise ship. (U.S. Coast Guard.)

The rescue swimmer is lowered onto the cruise ship as one of the ship's crew members turns his head away from the blast of the rotor wash. Even when the patient or survivor is not in the water, the rescue swimmer is frequently lowered first to help coordinate the on-deck preparations for the hoist. (U.S. Coast Guard.)

The sun sets.